The Road Not Taken and other Selected Poems

Robert Frost

©2011 Wilder Publications

Wilder Publications, Inc.
PO Box 10641
Blacksburg, VA 24063

ISBN 10: 1-61720-265-7
ISBN 13: 978-1-61720-265-0
First Edition

10 9 8 7 6 5 4 3 2 1

Contents

The Road Not Taken

Two roads diverged in a yellow wood,
And sorry I could not travel both
And be one traveler, long I stood
And looked down one as far as I could
To where it bent in the undergrowth;
Then took the other, as just as fair,
And having perhaps the better claim,
Because it was grassy and wanted wear;
Though as for that, the passing there
Had worn them really about the same,
And both that morning equally lay
In leaves no step had trodden black.
Oh, I kept the first for another day!
Yet knowing how way leads to way,
I doubted if I should ever come back.
I shall be telling this with a sigh
Somewhere ages and ages hence:
Two roads diverged in a wood, and I-
I took the one less traveled by,
And that has made all the difference.

The Death Of The Hired Man

MARY sat musing on the lamp-flame at the table
Waiting for Warren. When she heard his step,
She ran on tip-toe down the darkened passage
To meet him in the doorway with the news
And put him on his guard. "Silas is back."
She pushed him outward with her through the door
And shut it after her. "Be kind," she said.
She took the market things from Warren's arms
And set them on the porch, then drew him down
To sit beside her on the wooden steps.
"When was I ever anything but kind to him?
But I'll not have the fellow back," he said.
"I told him so last haying, didn't I?
'If he left then,' I said, 'that ended it.'
What good is he? Who else will harbour him
At his age for the little he can do?
What help he is there's no depending on.
Off he goes always when I need him most.
'He thinks he ought to earn a little pay,
Enough at least to buy tobacco with,
So he won't have to beg and be beholden.'
'All right,' I say, 'I can't afford to pay
Any fixed wages, though I wish I could.'
'Someone else can.' 'Then someone else will have to.'
I shouldn't mind his bettering himself
If that was what it was. You can be certain,
When he begins like that, there's someone at him
Trying to coax him off with pocket-money,—
In haying time, when any help is scarce.
In winter he comes back to us. I'm done."
"Sh! not so loud: he'll hear you," Mary said.
"I want him to: he'll have to soon or late."
"He's worn out. He's asleep beside the stove.
When I came up from Rowe's I found him here,
Huddled against the barn-door fast asleep,
A miserable sight, and frightening, too—
You needn't smile—I didn't recognise him—
I wasn't looking for him—and he's changed.

Wait till you see."
"Where did you say he'd been?"
"He didn't say. I dragged him to the house,
And gave him tea and tried to make him smoke.
I tried to make him talk about his travels.
Nothing would do: he just kept nodding off."
"What did he say? Did he say anything?"
"But little."
"Anything? Mary, confess
He said he'd come to ditch the meadow for me."
"Warren!"
"But did he? I just want to know."
"Of course he did. What would you have him say?
Surely you wouldn't grudge the poor old man
Some humble way to save his self-respect.
He added, if you really care to know,
He meant to clear the upper pasture, too.
That sounds like something you have heard before?
Warren, I wish you could have heard the way
He jumbled everything. I stopped to look
Two or three times—he made me feel so queer—
To see if he was talking in his sleep.
He ran on Harold Wilson—you remember—
The boy you had in haying four years since.
He's finished school, and teaching in his college.
Silas declares you'll have to get him back.
He says they two will make a team for work:
Between them they will lay this farm as smooth!
The way he mixed that in with other things.
He thinks young Wilson a likely lad, though daft
On education—you know how they fought
All through July under the blazing sun,
Silas up on the cart to build the load,
Harold along beside to pitch it on."
"Yes, I took care to keep well out of earshot."
"Well, those days trouble Silas like a dream.
You wouldn't think they would. How some things linger!
Harold's young college boy's assurance piqued him.
After so many years he still keeps finding
Good arguments he sees he might have used.

I sympathise. I know just how it feels
To think of the right thing to say too late.
Harold's associated in his mind with Latin.
He asked me what I thought of Harold's saying
He studied Latin like the violin
Because he liked it—that an argument!
He said he couldn't make the boy believe
He could find water with a hazel prong—
Which showed how much good school had ever done him.
He wanted to go over that. But most of all
He thinks if he could have another chance
To teach him how to build a load of hay—"
"I know, that's Silas' one accomplishment.
He bundles every forkful in its place,
And tags and numbers it for future reference,
So he can find and easily dislodge it
In the unloading. Silas does that well.
He takes it out in bunches like big birds' nests.
You never see him standing on the hay
He's trying to lift, straining to lift himself."
"He thinks if he could teach him that, he'd be
Some good perhaps to someone in the world.
He hates to see a boy the fool of books.
Poor Silas, so concerned for other folk,
And nothing to look backward to with pride,
And nothing to look forward to with hope,
So now and never any different."
Part of a moon was falling down the west,
Dragging the whole sky with it to the hills.
Its light poured softly in her lap. She saw
And spread her apron to it. She put out her hand
Among the harp-like morning-glory strings,
Taut with the dew from garden bed to eaves,
As if she played unheard the tenderness
That wrought on him beside her in the night.
"Warren," she said, "he has come home to die:
You needn't be afraid he'll leave you this time."
"Home," he mocked gently.
"Yes, what else but home?
It all depends on what you mean by home.

Of course he's nothing to us, any more
Than was the hound that came a stranger to us
Out of the woods, worn out upon the trail."
"Home is the place where, when you have to go there,
They have to take you in."
"I should have called it
Something you somehow haven't to deserve."
Warren leaned out and took a step or two,
Picked up a little stick, and brought it back
And broke it in his hand and tossed it by.
"Silas has better claim on us you think
Than on his brother? Thirteen little miles
As the road winds would bring him to his door.
Silas has walked that far no doubt to-day.
Why didn't he go there? His brother's rich,
A somebody–director in the bank."
"He never told us that."
"We know it though."
"I think his brother ought to help, of course.
I'll see to that if there is need. He ought of right
To take him in, and might be willing to—
He may be better than appearances.
But have some pity on Silas. Do you think
If he'd had any pride in claiming kin
Or anything he looked for from his brother,
He'd keep so still about him all this time?"
"I wonder what's between them."
"I can tell you.
Silas is what he is—we wouldn't mind him—
But just the kind that kinsfolk can't abide.
He never did a thing so very bad.
He don't know why he isn't quite as good
As anyone. He won't be made ashamed
To please his brother, worthless though he is."
"I can't think Si ever hurt anyone."
"No, but he hurt my heart the way he lay
And rolled his old head on that sharp-edged chair-back.
He wouldn't let me put him on the lounge.
You must go in and see what you can do.
I made the bed up for him there to-night.

8

You'll be surprised at him—how much he's broken.
His working days are done; I'm sure of it."
"I'd not be in a hurry to say that."
"I haven't been. Go, look, see for yourself.
But, Warren, please remember how it is:
He's come to help you ditch the meadow.
He has a plan. You mustn't laugh at him.
He may not speak of it, and then he may.
I'll sit and see if that small sailing cloud
Will hit or miss the moon."
It hit the moon.
Then there were three there, making a dim row,
The moon, the little silver cloud, and she.
Warren returned—too soon, it seemed to her,
Slipped to her side, caught up her hand and waited.
"Warren," she questioned.
"Dead," was all he answered.

The Mountain

THE mountain held the town as in a shadow
I saw so much before I slept there once:
I noticed that I missed stars in the west,
Where its black body cut into the sky.
Near me it seemed: I felt it like a wall
Behind which I was sheltered from a wind.
And yet between the town and it I found,
When I walked forth at dawn to see new things,
Were fields, a river, and beyond, more fields.
The river at the time was fallen away,
And made a widespread brawl on cobble-stones;
But the signs showed what it had done in spring;
Good grass-land gullied out, and in the grass
Ridges of sand, and driftwood stripped of bark.
I crossed the river and swung round the mountain.
And there I met a man who moved so slow
With white-faced oxen in a heavy cart,
It seemed no hand to stop him altogether.
"What town is this?" I asked.
        "This? Lunenburg."
Then I was wrong: the town of my sojourn,
Beyond the bridge, was not that of the mountain,
But only felt at night its shadowy presence.
"Where is your village? Very far from here?"
"There is no village—only scattered farms.
We were but sixty voters last election.
We can't in nature grow to many more:
That thing takes all the room!" He moved his goad.
The mountain stood there to be pointed at.
Pasture ran up the side a little way,
And then there was a wall of trees with trunks:
After that only tops of trees, and cliffs
Imperfectly concealed among the leaves.
A dry ravine emerged from under boughs
Into the pasture.
        "That looks like a path.
Is that the way to reach the top from here?—
Not for this morning, but some other time:

I must be getting back to breakfast now."
"I don't advise your trying from this side.
There is no proper path, but those that have
Been up, I understand, have climbed from Ladd's.
That's five miles back. You can't mistake the place:
They logged it there last winter some way up.
I'd take you, but I'm bound the other way."
"You've never climbed it?"
"I've been on the sides
Deer-hunting and trout-fishing. There's a brook
That starts up on it somewhere—I've heard say
Right on the top, tip-top—a curious thing.
But what would interest you about the brook,
It's always cold in summer, warm in winter.
One of the great sights going is to see
It steam in winter like an ox's breath,
Until the bushes all along its banks
Are inch-deep with the frosty spines and bristles—
You know the kind. Then let the sun shine on it!"
"There ought to be a view around the world
From such a mountain—if it isn't wooded
Clear to the top." I saw through leafy screens
Great granite terraces in sun and shadow,
Shelves one could rest a knee on getting up—
With depths behind him sheer a hundred feet;
Or turn and sit on and look out and down,
With little ferns in crevices at his elbow.
"As to that I can't say. But there's the spring,
Right on the summit, almost like a fountain.
That ought to be worth seeing."
"If it's there.
You never saw it?"
"I guess there's no doubt
About its being there. I never saw it.
It may not be right on the very top:
It wouldn't have to be a long way down
To have some head of water from above,
And a good distance down might not be noticed
By anyone who'd come a long way up.
One time I asked a fellow climbing it

To look and tell me later how it was."
"What did he say?"
"He said there was a lake
Somewhere in Ireland on a mountain top."
"But a lake's different. What about the spring?"
"He never got up high enough to see.
That's why I don't advise your trying this side.
He tried this side. I've always meant to go
And look myself, but you know how it is:
It doesn't seem so much to climb a mountain
You've worked around the foot of all your life.
What would I do? Go in my overalls,
With a big stick, the same as when the cows
Haven't come down to the bars at milking time?
Or with a shotgun for a stray black bear?
'Twouldn't seem real to climb for climbing it."
"I shouldn't climb it if I didn't want to—
Not for the sake of climbing. What's its name?"
"We call it Hor: I don't know if that's right."
"Can one walk around it? Would it be too far?"
"You can drive round and keep in Lunenburg,
But it's as much as ever you can do,
The boundary lines keep in so close to it.
Hor is the township, and the township's Hor—
And a few houses sprinkled round the foot,
Like boulders broken off the upper cliff,
Rolled out a little farther than the rest."
"Warm in December, cold in June, you say?"
"I don't suppose the water's changed at all.
You and I know enough to know it's warm
Compared with cold, and cold compared with warm.
But all the fun's in how you say a thing."
"You've lived here all your life?"
"Ever since Hor
Was no bigger than a—" What, I did not hear.
He drew the oxen toward him with light touches
Of his slim goad on nose and offside flank,
Gave them their marching orders and was moving.

FIRE AND ICE

Some say the world will end in fire,
Some say in ice.
From what I've tasted of desire
I hold with those who favor fire.
But if it had to perish twice,
I think I know enough of hate
To know that for destruction ice
Is also great,
And would suffice.

The Generations Of Men

A GOVERNOR it was proclaimed this time,
When all who would come seeking in New Hampshire
Ancestral memories might come together.
And those of the name Stark gathered in Bow,
A rock-strewn town where farming has fallen off,
And sprout-lands flourish where the axe has gone.
Someone had literally run to earth
In an old cellar hole in a by-road
The origin of all the family there.
Thence they were sprung, so numerous a tribe
That now not all the houses left in town
Made shift to shelter them without the help
Of here and there a tent in grove and orchard.
They were at Bow, but that was not enough:
Nothing would do but they must fix a day
To stand together on the crater's verge
That turned them on the world, and try to fathom
The past and get some strangeness out of it.
But rain spoiled all. The day began uncertain,
With clouds low trailing and moments of rain that misted.
The young folk held some hope out to each other
Till well toward noon when the storm settled down
With a swish in the grass. "What if the others
Are there," they said. "It isn't going to rain."
Only one from a farm not far away
Strolled thither, not expecting he would find
Anyone else, but out of idleness.
One, and one other, yes, for there were two.
The second round the curving hillside road
Was a girl; and she halted some way off
To reconnoitre, and then made up her mind
At least to pass by and see who he was,
And perhaps hear some word about the weather.
This was some Stark she didn't know. He nodded.
"No fête to-day," he said.
"It looks that way."
She swept the heavens, turning on her heel.
"I only idled down."

"I idled down."
Provision there had been for just such meeting
Of stranger cousins, in a family tree
Drawn on a sort of passport with the branch
Of the one bearing it done in detail—
Some zealous one's laborious device.
She made a sudden movement toward her bodice,
As one who clasps her heart. They laughed together.
"Stark?" he inquired. "No matter for the proof."
"Yes, Stark. And you?"
"I'm Stark." He drew his passport.
"You know we might not be and still be cousins:
The town is full of Chases, Lowes, and Baileys,
All claiming some priority in Starkness.
My mother was a Lane, yet might have married
Anyone upon earth and still her children
Would have been Starks, and doubtless here to-day."
"You riddle with your genealogy
Like a Viola. I don't follow you."
"I only mean my mother was a Stark
Several times over, and by marrying father
No more than brought us back into the name."
"One ought not to be thrown into confusion
By a plain statement of relationship,
But I own what you say makes my head spin.
You take my card—you seem so good at such things—
And see if you can reckon our cousinship.
Why not take seats here on the cellar wall
And dangle feet among the raspberry vines?"
"Under the shelter of the family tree."
"Just so—that ought to be enough protection."
"Not from the rain. I think it's going to rain."
"It's raining."
"No, it's misting; let's be fair.
Does the rain seem to you to cool the eyes?"
The situation was like this: the road
Bowed outward on the mountain half-way up,
And disappeared and ended not far off.
No one went home that way. The only house
Beyond where they were was a shattered seedpod.

15

And below roared a brook hidden in trees,
The sound of which was silence for the place.
This he sat listening to till she gave judgment.
"On father's side, it seems, we're—let me see—"
"Don't be too technical.—You have three cards."
"Four cards, one yours, three mine, one for each branch
Of the Stark family I'm a member of."
"D'you know a person so related to herself
Is supposed to be mad."
"I may be mad."
"You look so, sitting out here in the rain
Studying genealogy with me
You never saw before. What will we come to
With all this pride of ancestry, we Yankees?
I think we're all mad. Tell me why we're here
Drawn into town about this cellar hole
Like wild geese on a lake before a storm?
What do we see in such a hole, I wonder."
"The Indians had a myth of Chicamoztoc,
Which means The Seven Caves that We Came out of.
This is the pit from which we Starks were digged."
"You must be learned. That's what you see in it?"
"And what do you see?"
"Yes, what do I see?
First let me look. I see raspberry vines—"
"Oh, if you're going to use your eyes, just hear
What I see. It's a little, little boy,
As pale and dim as a match flame in the sun;
He's groping in the cellar after jam,
He thinks it's dark and it's flooded with daylight."
"He's nothing. Listen. When I lean like this
I can make out old Grandsir Stark distinctly,—
With his pipe in his mouth and his brown jug—
Bless you, it isn't Grandsir Stark, it's Granny,
But the pipe's there and smoking and the jug.
She's after cider, the old girl, she's thirsty;
Here's hoping she gets her drink and gets out safely."
"Tell me about her. Does she look like me?"
"She should, shouldn't she, you're so many times
Over descended from her. I believe

She does look like you. Stay the way you are.
The nose is just the same, and so's the chin—
Making allowance, making due allowance."
"You poor, dear, great, great, great, great Granny!"
"See that you get her greatness right. Don't stint her."
"Yes, it's important, though you think it isn't.
I won't be teased. But see how wet I am."
"Yes, you must go; we can't stay here for ever.
But wait until I give you a hand up.
A bead of silver water more or less
Strung on your hair won't hurt your summer looks.
I wanted to try something with the noise
That the brook raises in the empty valley.
We have seen visions—now consult the voices.
Something I must have learned riding in trains
When I was young. I used the roar
To set the voices speaking out of it,
Speaking or singing, and the band-music playing.
Perhaps you have the art of what I mean.
I've never listened in among the sounds
That a brook makes in such a wild descent.
It ought to give a purer oracle."
"It's as you throw a picture on a screen:
The meaning of it all is out of you;
The voices give you what you wish to hear."
"Strangely, it's anything they wish to give."
"Then I don't know. It must be strange enough.
I wonder if it's not your make-believe.
What do you think you're like to hear to-day?"
"From the sense of our having been together—
But why take time for what I'm like to hear?
I'll tell you what the voices really say.
You will do very well right where you are
A little longer. I mustn't feel too hurried,
Or I can't give myself to hear the voices."
"Is this some trance you are withdrawing into?"
"You must be very still; you mustn't talk."
"I'll hardly breathe."
"The voices seem to say—"
"I'm waiting."

"Don't! The voices seem to say:
Call her Nausicaa, the unafraid
Of an acquaintance made adventurously."
"I let you say that—on consideration."
"I don't see very well how you can help it.
You want the truth. I speak but by the voices.
You see they know I haven't had your name,
Though what a name should matter between us—"
"I shall suspect—"
"Be good. The voices say:
Call her Nausicaa, and take a timber
That you shall find lies in the cellar charred
Among the raspberries, and hew and shape it
For a door-sill or other corner piece
In a new cottage on the ancient spot.
The life is not yet all gone out of it.
And come and make your summer dwelling here,
And perhaps she will come, still unafraid,
And sit before you in the open door
With flowers in her lap until they fade,
But not come in across the sacred sill—"
"I wonder where your oracle is tending.
You can see that there's something wrong with it,
Or it would speak in dialect. Whose voice
Does it purport to speak in? Not old Grandsir's
Nor Granny's, surely. Call up one of them.
They have best right to be heard in this place."
"You seem so partial to our great-grandmother
(Nine times removed. Correct me if I err.)
You will be likely to regard as sacred
Anything she may say. But let me warn you,
Folks in her day were given to plain speaking.
You think you'd best tempt her at such a time?"
"It rests with us always to cut her off."
"Well then, it's Granny speaking: 'I dunnow!
Mebbe I'm wrong to take it as I do.
There ain't no names quite like the old ones though,
Nor never will be to my way of thinking.
One mustn't bear too hard on the new comers,
But there's a dite too many of them for comfort.

I should feel easier if I could see
More of the salt wherewith they're to be salted.
Son, you do as you're told! You take the timber—
It's as sound as the day when it was cut—
And begin over—' There, she'd better stop.
You can see what is troubling Granny, though.
But don't you think we sometimes make too much
Of the old stock? What counts is the ideals,
And those will bear some keeping still about."
"I can see we are going to be good friends."
"I like your 'going to be.' You said just now
It's going to rain."
"I know, and it was raining.
I let you say all that. But I must go now."
"You let me say it? on consideration?
How shall we say good-bye in such a case?"
"How shall we?"
"Will you leave the way to me?"
"No, I don't trust your eyes. You've said enough.
Now give me your hand up.—Pick me that flower."
"Where shall we meet again?"
"Nowhere but here
Once more before we meet elsewhere."
"In rain?"
"It ought to be in rain. Sometime in rain.
In rain to-morrow, shall we, if it rains?
But if we must, in sunshine." So she went.

THE GRINDSTONE

Having a wheel and four legs of its own
Has never availed the cumbersome grindstone
To get it anywhere that I can see.
These hands have helped it go and even race;
Not all the motion, though, they ever lent,
Not all the miles it may have thought it went,
Have got it one step from the starting place.
It stands beside the same old apple tree.
The shadow of the apple tree is thin
Upon it now; its feet are fast in snow.
All other farm machinery's gone in,
And some of it on no more legs and wheel
Than the grindstone can boast to stand or go.
(I'm thinking chiefly of the wheelbarrow.)
For months it hasn't known the taste of steel,
Washed down with rusty water in a tin.
But standing outdoors, hungry, in the cold,
Except in towns, at night, is not a sin.
And, anyway, its standing in the yard
Under a ruinous live apple tree
Has nothing any more to do with me,
Except that I remember how of old,
One summer day, all day I drove it hard,
And some one mounted on it rode it hard,
And he and I between us ground a blade.

I gave it the preliminary spin,
And poured on water (tears it might have been);
And when it almost gayly jumped and flowed,
A Father-Time-like man got on and rode,
Armed with a scythe and spectacles that glowed.
He turned on will-power to increase the load
And slow me down—and I abruptly slowed,
Like coming to a sudden railroad station.
I changed from hand to hand in desperation.

I wondered what machine of ages gone
This represented an improvement on.

For all I knew it may have sharpened spears
And arrowheads itself.
Much use for years Had gradually worn it an oblate
Spheroid that kicked and struggled in its gait,
Appearing to return me hate for hate.
(But I forgive it now as easily
As any other boyhood enemy
Whose pride has failed to get him anywhere.)
I wondered who it was the man thought ground—
The one who held the wheel back or the one
Who gave his life to keep it going round?
I wondered if he really thought it fair
For him to have the say when we were done.
Such were the bitter thoughts to which I turned.

Not for myself was I so much concerned.
Oh, no!—although, of course, I could have found
A better way to pass the afternoon
Than grinding discord out of a grindstone,
And beating insects at their gritty tune.
Nor was I for the man so much concerned.
Once when the grindstone almost jumped its bearing
It looked as if he might be badly thrown
And wounded on his blade. So far from caring,
I laughed inside, and only cranked the faster,
(It ran as if it wasn't greased but glued);
I welcomed any moderate disaster
That might be calculated to postpone
What evidently nothing could conclude.

The thing that made me more and more afraid
Was that we'd ground it sharp and hadn't known,
And now were only wasting precious blade.
And when he raised it dripping once and tried
The creepy edge of it with wary touch,
And viewed it over his glasses funny-eyed,
Only disinterestedly to decide
It needed a turn more, I could have cried
Wasn't there danger of a turn too much?
Mightn't we make it worse instead of better?

I was for leaving something to the whetter.
What if it wasn't all it should be?
I'd Be satisfied if he'd be satisfied.

THE WITCH OF COÖS

I staid the night for shelter at a farm
Behind the mountain, with a mother and son,
Two old-believers. They did all the talking.

The Mother
Folks think a witch who has familiar spirits
She could call up to pass a winter evening,
But won't, should be burned at the stake or something.
Summoning spirits isn't "Button, button,
Who's got the button?" I'd have you understand.

The Son
Mother can make a common table rear
And kick with two legs like an army mule.

The Mother
And when I've done it, what good have I done?
Rather than tip a table for you, let me
Tell you what Ralle the Sioux Control once told me.
He said the dead had souls, but when I asked him
How that could be—I thought the dead were souls,
He broke my trance. Don't that make you suspicious
That there's something the dead are keeping back?
Yes, there's something the dead are keeping back.

The Son
You wouldn't want to tell him what we have
Up attic, mother?

The Mother
Bones—a skeleton.

The Son
But the headboard of mother's bed is pushed
Against the attic door: the door is nailed.
It's harmless. Mother hears it in the night
Halting perplexed behind the barrier
Of door and headboard. Where it wants to get

Is back into the cellar where it came from.

The Mother
    We'll never let them, will we, son? We'll never!

The Son
    It left the cellar forty years ago
    And carried itself like a pile of dishes
    Up one flight from the cellar to the kitchen,
    Another from the kitchen to the bedroom,
Another from the bedroom to the attic,
    Right past both father and mother, and neither stopped it.
    Father had gone upstairs; mother was downstairs.
    I was a baby: I don't know where I was.

The Mother
    The only fault my husband found with me—
    I went to sleep before I went to bed,
    Especially in winter when the bed
    Might just as well be ice and the clothes snow.
    The night the bones came up the cellar-stairs
    Toffile had gone to bed alone and left me,
    But left an open door to cool the room off
    So as to sort of turn me out of it.
    I was just coming to myself enough
    To wonder where the cold was coming from,
    When I heard Toffile upstairs in the bedroom
    And thought I heard him downstairs in the cellar.
    The board we had laid down to walk dry-shod on
    When there was water in the cellar in spring
    Struck the hard cellar bottom. And then some one
    Began the stairs, two footsteps for each step,
    The way a man with one leg and a crutch,
    Or little child, comes up. It wasn't
    Toffile: It wasn't any one who could be there.
    The bulkhead double-doors were double-locked
    And swollen tight and buried under snow.
    The cellar windows were banked up with sawdust
    And swollen tight and buried under snow.
    It was the bones. I knew them—and good reason.

My first impulse was to get to the knob
And hold the door. But the bones didn't try
The door; they halted helpless on the landing,
Waiting for things to happen in their favor.
The faintest restless rustling ran all through them.
I never could have done the thing I did
If the wish hadn't been too strong in me
To see how they were mounted for this walk.
I had a vision of them put together
Not like a man, but like a chandelier.
So suddenly I flung the door wide on him.
A moment he stood balancing with emotion,
And all but lost himself. (A tongue of fire
Flashed out and licked along his upper teeth.
Smoke rolled inside the sockets of his eyes.)
Then he came at me with one hand outstretched,
The way he did in life once; but this time
I struck the hand off brittle on the floor,
And fell back from him on the floor myself.
The finger-pieces slid in all directions.
(Where did I see one of those pieces lately?
Hand me my button-box—it must be there.)
I sat up on the floor and shouted, "Toffile,
It's coming up to you." It had its choice
Of the door to the cellar or the hall.
It took the hall door for the novelty,
And set off briskly for so slow a thing,
Still going every which way in the joints, though,
So that it looked like lightning or a scribble,
From the slap I had just now given its hand.
I listened till it almost climbed the stairs
From the hall to the only finished bedroom,
Before I got up to do anything;
Then ran and shouted, "Shut the bedroom door,
Toffile, for my sake!" "Company," he said,
"Don't make me get up; I'm too warm in bed."
So lying forward weakly on the handrail
I pushed myself upstairs, and in the light
(The kitchen had been dark) I had to own
I could see nothing. "Toffile, I don't see it.

It's with us in the room, though. It's the bones."
"What bones?" "The cellar bones—out of the grave."

That made him throw his bare legs out of bed
And sit up by me and take hold of me.
I wanted to put out the light and see
If I could see it, or else mow the room,
With our arms at the level of our knees,
And bring the chalk-pile down. "I'll tell you what—
It's looking for another door to try.
The uncommonly deep snow has made him think
Of his old song, The Wild Colonial Boy,
He always used to sing along the tote-road.
He's after an open door to get out-doors.
Let's trap him with an open door up attic."
Toffile agreed to that, and sure enough,
Almost the moment he was given an opening,
The steps began to climb the attic stairs.
I heard them. Toffile didn't seem to hear them.
"Quick!" I slammed to the door and held the knob.
"Toffile, get nails." I made him nail the door shut,
And push the headboard of the bed against it.

Then we asked was there anything
Up attic that we'd ever want again.
The attic was less to us than the cellar.
If the bones liked the attic, let them like it,
Let them stay in the attic. When they sometimes
Come down the stairs at night and stand perplexed
Behind the door and headboard of the bed,
Brushing their chalky skull with chalky fingers,
With sounds like the dry rattling of a shutter,
That's what I sit up in the dark to say—
To no one any more since Toffile died.
Let them stay in the attic since they went there.
I promised Toffile to be cruel to them
For helping them be cruel once to him.

The Son
We think they had a grave down in the cellar.

The Mother
   We know they had a grave down in the cellar.

The Son
   We never could find out whose bones they were.

The Mother
   Yes, we could too, son. Tell the truth for once.
   They were a man's his father killed for me.
   I mean a man he killed instead of me.
   The least I could do was to help dig their grave.
   We were about it one night in the cellar.
   Son knows the story: but 'twas not for him
   To tell the truth, suppose the time had come.
   Son looks surprised to see me end a lie
   We'd kept up all these years between ourselves
   So as to have it ready for outsiders.
   But to-night I don't care enough to lie—
   I don't remember why I ever cared.
   Toffile, if he were here, I don't believe
   Could tell you why he ever cared himself....

   She hadn't found the finger-bone she wanted
   Among the buttons poured out in her lap.

   I verified the name next morning: Toffile;
   The rural letter-box said Toffile Lajway.

A BROOK IN THE CITY

The farm house lingers, though averse to square
With the new city street it has to wear
A number in. But what about the brook
That held the house as in an elbow-crook?
I ask as one who knew the brook, its strength
And impulse, having dipped a finger-length
And made it leap my knuckle, having tossed
A flower to try its currents where they crossed.
The meadow grass could be cemented down
From growing under pavements of a town;
The apple trees be sent to hearth-stone flame.
Is water wood to serve a brook the same?
How else dispose of an immortal force
No longer needed? Staunch it at its source
With cinder loads dumped down? The brook was thrown
Deep in a sewer dungeon under stone
In fetid darkness still to live and run—
And all for nothing it had ever done
Except forget to go in fear perhaps.
No one would know except for ancient maps
That such a brook ran water. But I wonder I
f, from its being kept forever under,
These thoughts may not have risen that so keep
This new-built city from both work and sleep.

Design

I found a dimpled spider, fat and white,
On a white heal-all, holding up a moth
Like a white piece of rigid satin cloth—
Assorted characters of death and blight
Mixed ready to begin the morning right,
Like the ingredients of a witches' broth—
A snow-drop spider, a flower like froth,
And dead wings carried like a paper kite.

What had that flower to do with being white,
The wayside blue and innocent heal-all?
What brought the kindred spider to that height,
Then steered the white moth thither in the night?
What but design of darkness to appal?—
If design govern in a thing so small.

House Fear

Always—I tell you this they learned—
Always at night when they returned
To the lonely house from far away
To lamps unlighted and fire gone gray,
They learned to rattle the lock and key
To give whatever might chance to be
Warning and time to be off in flight:
And preferring the out- to the in-door night,
They learned to leave the house-door wide
Until they had lit the lamp inside.

The Lockless Door

It went many years,
But at last came a knock,
And I thought of the door
With no lock to lock.

I blew out the light,
I tip-toed the floor,
And raised both hands
In prayer to the door.

But the knock came again
My window was wide;
I climbed on the sill
And descended outside.

Back over the sill
I bade a "Come in"
To whoever the knock
At the door may have been.

So at a knock
I emptied my cage
To hide in the world
And alter with age.

Storm Fear

When the wind works against us in the dark,
And pelts with snow
The lower chamber window on the east,
And whispers with a sort of stifled bark,
The beast,
'Come out! Come out!'—
It costs no inward struggle not to go,
Ah, no!
I count our strength,
Two and a child,
Those of us not asleep subdued to mark
How the cold creeps as the fire dies at length,—
How drifts are piled,
Dooryard and road ungraded,
Till even the comforting barn grows far away,
And my heart owns a doubt
Whether 'tis in us to arise with day
And save ourselves unaided.

Snow

The three stood listening to a fresh access
Of wind that caught against the house a moment,
Gulped snow, and then blew free again-the Coles
Dressed, but dishevelled from some hours of sleep,
Meserve belittled in the great skin coat he wore.

Meserve was first to speak. He pointed backward
Over his shoulder with his pipe-stem, saying,
"You can just see it glancing off the roof
Making a great scroll upward toward the sky,
Long enough for recording all our names on.-
I think I'll just call up my wife and tell her
I'm here-so far-and starting on again.
I'll call her softly so that if she's wise
And gone to sleep, she needn't wake to answer."
Three times he barely stirred the bell, then listened.
"Why, Lett, still up? Lett, I'm at Cole's. I'm late.
I called you up to say Good-night from here
Before I went to say Good-morning there.-
I thought I would.- I know, but, Lett-I know-
I could, but what's the sense? The rest won't be
So bad.- Give me an hour for it.- Ho, ho,
Three hours to here! But that was all up hill;
The rest is down.- Why no, no, not a wallow:
They kept their heads and took their time to it
Like darlings, both of them. They're in the barn.-
My dear, I'm coming just the same. I didn't
Call you to ask you to invite me home.-"
He lingered for some word she wouldn't say,
Said it at last himself, "Good-night," and then,
Getting no answer, closed the telephone.
The three stood in the lamplight round the table
With lowered eyes a moment till he said,
"I'll just see how the horses are."

"Yes, do,"
Both the Coles said together. Mrs. Cole
Added: "You can judge better after seeing.-

I want you here with me, Fred. Leave him here,
Brother Meserve. You know to find your way
Out through the shed."

"I guess I know my way,
I guess I know where I can find my name
Carved in the shed to tell me who I am
If it don't tell me where I am. I used
To play-"

"You tend your horses and come back.
Fred Cole, you're going to let him!"

"Well, aren't you?
How can you help yourself?"

"I called him Brother.
Why did I call him that?"

"It's right enough.
That's all you ever heard him called round here.
He seems to have lost off his Christian name."

"Christian enough I should call that myself.
He took no notice, did he? Well, at least
I didn't use it out of love of him,
The dear knows. I detest the thought of him
With his ten children under ten years old.
I hate his wretched little Racker Sect,
All's ever I heard of it, which isn't much.
But that's not saying-Look, Fred Cole, it's twelve,
Isn't it, now? He's been here half an hour.
He says he left the village store at nine.
Three hours to do four miles-a mile an hour
Or not much better. Why, it doesn't seem
As if a man could move that slow and move.
Try to think what he did with all that time.
And three miles more to go!"
"Don't let him go.
Stick to him, Helen. Make him answer you.

34

That sort of man talks straight on all his life
From the last thing he said himself, stone deaf
To anything anyone else may say.
I should have thought, though, you could make him hear you."

"What is he doing out a night like this?
Why can't he stay at home?"

"He had to preach."

"It's no night to be out."

"He may be small,
He may be good, but one thing's sure, he's tough."

"And strong of stale tobacco."

"He'll pull through.'
"You only say so. Not another house
Or shelter to put into from this place
To theirs. I'm going to call his wife again."

"Wait and he may. Let's see what he will do.
Let's see if he will think of her again.
But then I doubt he's thinking of himself
He doesn't look on it as anything."

"He shan't go-there!"

"It is a night, my dear."

"One thing: he didn't drag God into it."

"He don't consider it a case for God."

"You think so, do you? You don't know the kind.
He's getting up a miracle this minute.
Privately-to himself, right now, he's thinking
He'll make a case of it if he succeeds,
But keep still if he fails."

"Keep still all over.
He'll be dead-dead and buried."

"Such a trouble!
Not but I've every reason not to care
What happens to him if it only takes
Some of the sanctimonious conceit
Out of one of those pious scalawags."

"Nonsense to that! You want to see him safe."

"You like the runt."

"Don't you a little?"

"Well,
I don't like what he's doing, which is what
You like, and like him for."

"Oh, yes you do.
You like your fun as well as anyone;
Only you women have to put these airs on
To impress men. You've got us so ashamed
Of being men we can't look at a good fight
Between two boys and not feel bound to stop it.
Let the man freeze an ear or two, I say.-
He's here. I leave him all to you. Go in
And save his life.- All right, come in, Meserve.
Sit down, sit down. How did you find the horses?"

"Fine, fine."

"And ready for some more? My wife here
Says it won't do. You've got to give it up."

"Won't you to please me? Please! If I say please?
Mr. Meserve, I'll leave it to your wife.
What did your wife say on the telephone?"

Meserve seemed to heed nothing but the lamp

Or something not far from it on the table.
By straightening out and lifting a forefinger,
He pointed with his hand from where it lay
Like a white crumpled spider on his knee:
"That leaf there in your open book! It moved
Just then, I thought. It's stood erect like that,
There on the table, ever since I came,
Trying to turn itself backward or forward,
I've had my eye on it to make out which;
If forward, then it's with a friend's impatience-
You see I know-to get you on to things
It wants to see how you will take, if backward
It's from regret for something you have passed
And failed to see the good of. Never mind,
Things must expect to come in front of us
A many times-I don't say just how many-
That varies with the things-before we see them.
One of the lies would make it out that nothing
Ever presents itself before us twice.
Where would we be at last if that were so?
Our very life depends on everything's
Recurring till we answer from within.
The thousandth time may prove the charm.- That leaf!
It can't turn either way. It needs the wind's help.
But the wind didn't move it if it moved.
It moved itself. The wind's at naught in here.
It couldn't stir so sensitively poised
A thing as that. It couldn't reach the lamp
To get a puff of black smoke from the flame,
Or blow a rumple in the collie's coat.
You make a little foursquare block of air,
Quiet and light and warm, in spite of all
The illimitable dark and cold and storm,
And by so doing give these three, lamp, dog,
And book-leaf, that keep near you, their repose;
Though for all anyone can tell, repose
May be the thing you haven't, yet you give it.
So false it is that what we haven't we can't give;
So false, that what we always say is true.
I'll have to turn the leaf if no one else will.

It won't lie down. Then let it stand. Who cares?"

"I shouldn't want to hurry you, Meserve,
But if you're going- Say you'll stay, you know?
But let me raise this curtain on a scene,
And show you how it's piling up against you.
You see the snow-white through the white of frost?
Ask Helen how far up the sash it's climbed
Since last we read the gage."

"It looks as if
Some pallid thing had squashed its features flat
And its eyes shut with overeagerness
To see what people found so interesting
In one another, and had gone to sleep
Of its own stupid lack of understanding,
Or broken its white neck of mushroom stuff
Short off, and died against the window-pane."

"Brother Meserve, take care, you'll scare yourself
More than you will us with such nightmare talk.
It's you it matters to, because it's you
Who have to go out into it alone."

"Let him talk, Helen, and perhaps he'll stay."

"Before you drop the curtain-I'm reminded:
You recollect the boy who came out here
To breathe the air one winter-had a room
Down at the Averys'? Well, one sunny morning
After a downy storm, he passed our place
And found me banking up the house with snow.
And I was burrowing in deep for warmth,
Piling it well above the window-sills.
The snow against the window caught his eye.
'Hey, that's a pretty thought'-those were his words.
'So you can think it's six feet deep outside,
While you sit warm and read up balanced rations.
You can't get too much winter in the winter.'
Those were his words. And he went home and all

38

But banked the daylight out of Avery's windows.
Now you and I would go to no such length.
At the same time you can't deny it makes
It not a mite worse, sitting here, we three,
Playing our fancy, to have the snowline run
So high across the pane outside. There where
There is a sort of tunnel in the frost
More like a tunnel than a hole-way down
At the far end of it you see a stir
And quiver like the frayed edge of the drift
Blown in the wind. I like that-I like that.
Well, now I leave you, people."

"Come, Meserve,
We thought you were deciding not to go-
The ways you found to say the praise of comfort
And being where you are. You want to stay."

"I'll own it's cold for such a fall of snow.
This house is frozen brittle, all except
This room you sit in. If you think the wind
Sounds further off, it's not because it's dying;
You're further under in the snow-that's all-
And feel it less. Hear the soft bombs of dust
It bursts against us at the chimney mouth,
And at the eaves. I like it from inside
More than I shall out in it. But the horses
Are rested and it's time to say good-night,
And let you get to bed again. Good-night,
Sorry I had to break in on your sleep."

"Lucky for you you did. Lucky for you
You had us for a half-way station
To stop at. If you were the kind of man
Paid heed to women, you'd take my advice
And for your family's sake stay where you are.
But what good is my saying it over and over?
You've done more than you had a right to think
You could do-now. You know the risk you take
In going on."

"Our snow-storms as a rule
Aren't looked on as man-killers, and although
I'd rather be the beast that sleeps the sleep
Under it all, his door sealed up and lost,
Than the man fighting it to keep above it,
Yet think of the small birds at roost and not
In nests. Shall I be counted less than they are?
Their bulk in water would be frozen rock
In no time out to-night. And yet to-morrow
They will come budding boughs from tree to tree
Flirting their wings and saying Chickadee,
As if not knowing what you meant by the word storm."

"But why when no one wants you to go on?
Your wife-she doesn't want you to. We don't,
And you yourself don't want to. Who else is there?"

"Save us from being cornered by a woman.
Well, there's"-She told Fred afterward that in
The pause right there, she thought the dreaded word
Was coming, "God." But no, he only said
"Well, there's-the storm. That says I must go on.
That wants me as a war might if it came.
Ask any man."

He threw her that as something
To last her till he got outside the door.
He had Cole with him to the barn to see him off.
When Cole returned he found his wife still standing
Beside the table near the open book,
Not reading it.

"Well, what kind of a man
Do you call that?" she said.

"He had the gift
Of words, or is it tongues, I ought to say?"

"Was ever such a man for seeing likeness?"

"Or disregarding people's civil questions-
What? We've found out in one hour more about him
Than we had seeing him pass by in the road
A thousand times. If that's the way he preaches!
You didn't think you'd keep him after all.
Oh, I'm not blaming you. He didn't leave you
Much say in the matter, and I'm just as glad
We're not in for a night of him. No sleep
If he had stayed. The least thing set him going.
It's quiet as an empty church without him."

"But how much better off are we as it is?
We'll have to sit here till we know he's safe."

"Yes, I suppose you'll want to, but I shouldn't.
He knows what he can do, or he wouldn't try.
Get into bed I say, and get some rest.
He won't come back, and if he telephones,
It won't be for an hour or two."

"Well then.
We can't be any help by sitting here
And living his fight through with him, I suppose."

Cole had been telephoning in the dark.
Mrs. Cole's voice came from an inner room:
"Did she call you or you call her?"

"She me.
You'd better dress: you won't go back to bed.
We must have been asleep: it's three and after."

"Had she been ringing long? I'll get my wrapper.
I want to speak to her."

"All she said was,
He hadn't come and had he really started."

"She knew he had, poor thing, two hours ago."

"He had the shovel. He'll have made a fight."

"Why did I ever let him leave this house!"

"Don't begin that. You did the best you could
To keep him-though perhaps you didn't quite
Conceal a wish to see him show the spunk
To disobey you. Much his wife'll thank you."

"Fred, after all I said! You shan't make out
That it was any way but what it was.
Did she let on by any word she said
She didn't thank me?"

"When I told her 'Gone,'
'Well then,' she said, and 'Well then'-like a threat.
And then her voice came scraping slow: 'Oh, you,
Why did you let him go'?"

"Asked why we let him?
You let me there. I'll ask her why she let him.
She didn't dare to speak when he was here.

Their number's-twenty-one? The thing won't work.
Someone's receiver's down. The handle stumbles.

The stubborn thing, the way it jars your arm!
It's theirs. She's dropped it from her hand and gone."

"Try speaking. Say 'Hello'!"

"Hello. Hello."

"What do you hear?"

"I hear an empty room-
You know-it sounds that way. And yes, I hear-
I think I hear a clock-and windows rattling.
No step though. If she's there she's sitting down."

"Shout, she may hear you."

"Shouting is no good."

"Keep speaking then."

"Hello. Hello. Hello.
You don't suppose-? She wouldn't go out doors?"

"I'm half afraid that's just what she might do."

"And leave the children?"

"Wait and call again.
You can't hear whether she has left the door
Wide open and the wind's blown out the lamp
And the fire's died and the room's dark and cold?"

"One of two things, either she's gone to bed
Or gone out doors."

"In which case both are lost.
Do you know what she's like? Have you ever met her?
It's strange she doesn't want to speak to us."

"Fred, see if you can hear what I hear. Come."

"A clock maybe."

"Don't you hear something else?"

"Not talking."
"No."

"Why, yes, I hear-what is it?"

"What do you say it is?"

"A baby's crying!
Frantic it sounds, though muffled and far off."

"Its mother wouldn't let it cry like that,
Not if she's there."

"What do you make of it?"

"There's only one thing possible to make,
That is, assuming that she has gone out.
Of course she hasn't though." They both sat down
Helpless. "There's nothing we can do till morning."

"Fred, I shan't let you think of going out."

"Hold on." The double bell began to chirp.
They started up. Fred took the telephone.
"Hello, Meserve. You're there, then!-And your wife?

Good! Why I asked-she didn't seem to answer.
He says she went to let him in the barn.-
We're glad. Oh, say no more about it, man.
Drop in and see us when you're passing."

"Well,
She has him then, though what she wants him for
I don't see."
"Possibly not for herself.
Maybe she only wants him for the children."

"The whole to-do seems to have been for nothing.
What spoiled our night was to him just his fun.
What did he come in for?-To talk and visit?
Thought he'd just call to tell us it was snowing.
If he thinks he is going to make our house
A halfway coffee house 'twixt town and nowhere—"

"I thought you'd feel you'd been too much concerned."

"You think you haven't been concerned yourself."

"If you mean he was inconsiderate
To rout us out to think for him at midnight

44

And then take our advice no more than nothing,
Why, I agree with you. But let's forgive him.
We've had a share in one night of his life.
What'll you bet he ever calls again?"

CPSIA information can be obtained at www.ICGtesting.com
Printed in the USA
LVOW121720020212

266764LV00004B/26/P